GAZZA
DAFT AS A BRUSH?

PAUL GASCOIGNE

Macdonald
Queen Anne Press

A QUEEN ANNE PRESS BOOK

© Paul Gascoigne 1989 and 1990

First published in Great Britain in hardcover in 1989 by
Queen Anne Press, a division of
Macdonald & Co (Publishers) Ltd
Orbit House
1 New Fetter Lane
London EC4A 1AR

A member of Maxwell Macmillan Pergamon Publishing Corporation

British Library Cataloguing in Publication Data
Gascoigne, Paul
   Gazza-daft as a brush?
   1. Great Britain. Association football
   I. Title
   796.334'0941

   ISBN 0-356-17977-X (hardcover)
        0-356-19751-4 (paperback)

Typeset by Cylinder Typesetting Limited, London

Printed and bound in Great Britain by Richard Clay Ltd, London and
Norwich

For my family
and for the people of Dunston,
who have given me
so much help and encouragement.

PICTURE CREDITS

Aerofilms Ltd 14-15, 48-9
All-Sport/Ben Radford 55
Associated Sports Photography 13, 40, 56, 79; ASP/Stuart D. Franklin 22, 34,
    35, 42-3, 83
Bob Thomas 7, 44, 62
Colorsport 17, 24, 25, 27, 50, 60-1, 63, 71 (right), 73, 76, 77, 78, 80, 81,
    86, 93 (left), 94
Doug Poole 47, 95
Gazza's Mum 10, 11
Rex Features 58
Sporting Pictures 20, 29, 31, 37, 57, 74, 75, 85, 90, 92
Syndication International Ltd 52, 53, 68, 71 (left), 93 (right)

All cartoons and jacket illustration by Mark Draisey.

Paul Gascoigne would like to thank his co-writer, Matthew Sturgis, for all his
help in the preparation of this book.

Macho of the Day.

20 THINGS YOU NEVER KNEW ABOUT GAZZA

(unless, of course, you did know them already.)

1 His favourite colour is light blue.
2 He was once caught, as an apprentice, drinking the dregs out of the sherry glasses in the players' lounge at Newcastle United.
3 He drives a blue Mercedes.
4 Southampton turned him down as a schoolboy trialist.
5 Mirandinha calls him 'The Crazy One'.
6 He was a schoolboy tennis star.
7 One of his favourite films is *The Naked Gun*.
8 He likes singing 'Love on the Rocks' by Neil Diamond.
9 He loves lobster.
10 He once lost half a stone in a week to win a £1 bet with the Newcastle coach Colin Suggett.
11 The Gascoigne family dog is an enormous Burmese Mountain Dog called Jason.
12 Jackie Milburn considered him the best young player he'd seen in 35 years.
13 He improved his stamina by training with Steve Cram's coach, Stan Long.
14 His middle name is Ignatius.
15 Fact 14 isn't true.
16 I just made it up to test you.
17 He plays for Tottenham Hotspur.
18 Everyone probably knows this already.
19 Well, very nearly everyone.
20 But I can't think of any more Gazza 'trivia'.

THE PAUL GASCOIGNE STORY

PART

1

By Jack McHack, Ghostwriter of the Year 1989

Paul Gascoigne was born in Gateshead, Newcastle, on 27 May 1967, the second in a family of four. He has a younger brother and two sisters. As a very young toddler Paul showed little interest in football, but for his fifth birthday his father bought him a ball and Paul fell in love with it. He played in the garden at home and his Dad would take him to the local park. By the age of seven Paul had developed such skills that the people of Newcastle, always keen judges of footballing skill and ready appreciators of free entertainment, would stop to admire his play.

Paul, amazing to relate, was very skinny as a young child. His Mum was so anxious about him that she even took him to the doctor. The doctor, after taking various measurements and readings, pronounced that for his age, height and build Paul was three-quarters of an ounce underweight. Impressive though this was, it was not good enough for Mrs Gascoigne; she wanted perfection. She soon fed him up to cover the missing three-quarters of an ounce. Paul would later go on to do considerably more.

At school Paul concentrated more on his football than on his books. 'I always knew I wanted to be a footballer. We'd play during break and at dinner-time.' Paul soon became aware of his rare skills and his equally rare lack of false modesty. 'Even at seven I used to think I was better than the other lads. The kids I was playing with were good, but I always wanted to improve myself. So my Dad got us into a Boys' Club, which I was a bit too young for. But my Dad told lies about my age. It was a very good club – football, just total football. I loved it!' Even though you were supposed to be ten to join the Redheugh Boys' Club team the eight-and-a-half-year-old Gazza was soon bustling about, controlling their midfield. 'By the time I was ten or eleven we had become unbeatable.'

From Redheugh Boys' Club Paul went on to play for the local district and his performance at that level landed him trials with several clubs – Middlesbrough (which had strong links with Redheugh), Newcastle, Southampton and Ipswich Town. 'Ipswich was a very good club. Bobby Robson was manager then. He was pleased with the way I played, and told me to keep doing the things I do well. But he thought I was too small, so he didn't put in for me.'

Paul, the schoolboy star, basks in the limelight (or is it the sunlight?)

Since then Gazza has certainly kept on doing the things he does best – winning the ball, running the play, making defenders look daft and scoring some fine goals. And now no one would think to call him too small. The advice was well taken. Gazza signed schoolboy forms with his home-town club, Newcastle United. And Bobby Robson would have to wait for a second chance to manage Gascoigne's precocious talents . . .

Paul (back row, left) has always been amongst the trophies.

WHAT'S IN A NAME

The name Gascoigne is French in origin. It is derived from Gascony, an area in south-western France. Gascony was famous for producing cheap wine and very brave soldiers.

But the Gascons were yet more famous for their boastfulness. They were great braggers, says my Dad.

Quite when and why some Gascons made their way from France to the north-east of England is unknown, but my family has lived in the area for some time.

Few people in Newcastle escape without some sort of a nickname and my Dad, John, was himself known as Gassa, as was his father before him.

The 'zz' in 'Gazza' came from an early schoolboy coach of mine. He came from near Sunderland and pronounced the name with a distinctive 'zz' sound. Pretty interesting, eh?

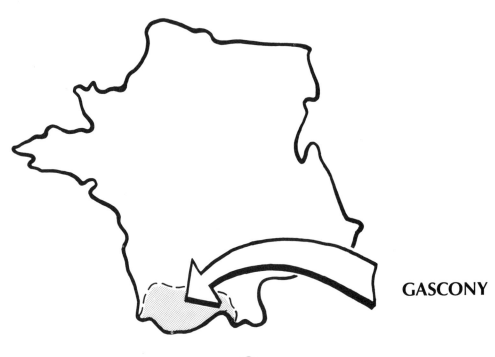

GASCONY

Remember: Try to come in on the blind side.

MY HOME TOWN

I really love Newcastle. They know about football there. The people are great. They are basically happy-go-lucky types. At first they were a bit unhappy that I'd left, but now, what with Newcastle United in the state it's in, they all say 'you've done the right thing'. It's always good to go back to Newcastle to see my family and my mates and to do some fishing.

Famous things that have come from Newcastle:
Coal
Lindisfarne
Jackie Milburn
The Venerable Bede
Viz
The Queen*
Newcastle Brown Ale
The Tyne

*This is not actually true – I put it in to make the list longer and give it a bit of added glamour – not that Newcastle Brown Ale isn't perfectly glamorous in its own right.

GAZZA'S DARKEST HOUR

As a young apprentice with Newcastle United one of my duties was to look after Kevin Keegan's football boots. Keegan, the former England captain, had made a surprise move to Second Division Newcastle and had soon become the darling of the Gallowgate and the inspiration of the rest of the team.

Looking after the boots of one of the country's most famous players was a great responsibility for me in my teenage years. It was also an exciting opportunity. I thought I was on to a good thing because I would be sure of a big tip at the end of the season.

But all too soon I was doubting whether I would even make it to the end of the season . . .

Sometimes an apprentice would have to break in a player's boots for him, wearing them around the house and garden. It was an accepted part of the job although it can't have been very good for my Mum's carpets.

One day Kevin gave me three pairs of boots to take home. I remember going back home on the Metro and showing them off to some of my mates. When I got home I discovered one of the boots was missing.

I panicked. Where had I left it? How could I find it? What might happen to me if I couldn't? I went back to the Metro and looked round all the stations. I was frantic. Then I went to the bus station to see if it had turned up there. It hadn't.

It was a very black moment. To have had the boot of the club's finest player in my care, and to have lost it . . . I was convinced I was going to get the sack.

I was so frightened I asked my Dad to explain to Kevin what had happened. Kevin was great, though. He told me he'd never really liked the boots anyway.

Kevin Keegan celebrates the loss of his football boot.

(17)

GAZZA'S TACTICAL TIPS

Soccer coaches now realise that football is an entertaining sport and that the best players are good entertainers as well as good footballers.

Although it is not necessary to be a trick-cyclist or a stand-up comedian to play the game well, you do need to appreciate the importance of the spectators. After-goal celebrations are a vital feature of football as entertainment. All players should learn to punch the air and run towards their own supporters' end of the ground when they score – unless, of course, it's an own goal.

Running 'off' the goal-scorer is also important. The scorer's team-mates should converge upon him as swiftly as possible to a) hug him, b) kiss him (on the cheek), c) punch the air, d) pat him on the back, e) slap his upheld palm.

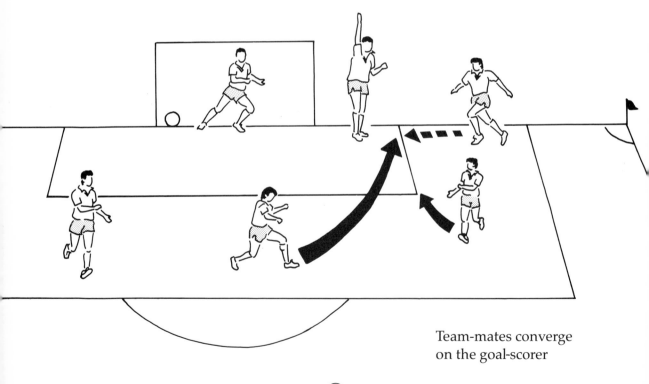

Team-mates converge
on the goal-scorer

The hand-slap

Remember: Football is a contact sport.

GAZZA'S TOP TEN

1 Do You Think I'm Gazza (Rod Stewart)
2 Radio Gazza (Queen)
3 Young, Gifted and Fat (Bob and Marcia)
4 Amazing Gaz (Royal Scots Dragoon Guards)
5 Gazzamatazz (Quincy Jones)
6 These Boots Are Made For Playing Football (Nancy Sinatra)
7 No One Quite Like Gazza (St Winifred's School Choir)
8 Life's a Gaz (T. Rex)
9 (White) Hart-lane Hotel (Elvis Presley)
10 Don't Stand So Close To Me (The Police, with Vinny Jones)

THE PERILS OF BEING A FOOTBALLER 1

WASPS

I've been stung by wasps a couple of times. Once was just on the arm. The other time was when I was still an apprentice up at Newcastle.

I was the substitute at a Reserves' match and was waiting on the touch-line when I was stung on the neck by one mad wasp. I started leaping around in pain and our coach had to come over and suck the sting out.

The television cameras were there, to film one of our lads who was playing, but at that point they decided to concentrate on me having my neck sucked; a real vampire movie.

And, as if that wasn't humiliating enough, I then had a great red love-bite on my neck for days afterwards. It was hard to explain to my girlfriend that I'd got it from the Reserve team coach.

SOCCER STARS

by Russell Grunt

Paul Gascoigne
Born 27/5/67

THE GEMINI FOOTBALLER

The sign of the twins is governed by Mercury, the planet of communication, so it is no surprise to discover that Gemini footballers shout a great deal.

But they don't only want to communicate with their own colleagues, they also want to have a rapport with the crowd. Geminis are great showmen – some might say show-offs – and the Gemini footballer is often the darling of the fans.

Their element is air, but this doesn't necessarily mean that they enjoy the punt-it-up-the-middle, long-ball game, or that they are good at heading the ball. The airiness of the Gemini footballer is more often revealed in his light-as-a-feather footwork and his flights of footballing fancy.

All those born under the sign of the twins have conflicting elements in their personality. Behind the extrovert showman there might lurk a sensitive and retiring spirit.

There are surprisingly few Gemini footballers but their calibre is often exceptional.

GEMINI PLAYERS: Alan Hansen, Mark Lawrenson, Peter Reid.

Mercurial talents: footballing 'twins'
Alan Hansen and Peter Reid.

CATCH OF THE DAY

After a relaxing morning at the training ground I like to get down to the serious business of fishing.

I carry my rods everywhere, and have had some good catches since moving south. I do a lot of fly fishing. I recently caught a six-pound bluebottle. And when I go back up north, I sometimes take a boat out. It's great up at New-castle, on the coast. I've been sea fishing a couple of times, but all I caught was 'flu.

Skill, concentration, judgement and guts are necessary for successful fishing. To the untutored eye it might appear that the fisherman is just standing beside a gently flowing stream, untroubled by the cares of the world, content to listen to the chirrup of the birds and the swish of the wind in the trees. But, in fact, a world of care rages behind his unruffled façade. Fishing is not as easy as it looks. No way.

First, you have to remember to bring your fishing rods. You have to take care not to wade in over the top of your wellingtons. You have to be prepared to stand quietly, lost in the depths of the tranquil countryside, for long periods of time. Also you have to be prepared to beat out a fish's brains on a flat stone and take out its insides with a pen-knife. Fishing takes guts.

Football is, of course, a great preparation for the rigours of fishing. Anyone would learn patience standing, unmarked, in the middle of a football field, waiting for Chris Waddle to pass. And there is little that a game up against John 'Fash the Bash' Fashanu won't teach you about beating the brains out of things. Fishing, as they say, is a funny old game.

Precision play. Gazza tests the wind-speed before floating a free kick into the area.

A NOTE TO CHILDREN (AND POPEYE)

As a kid I was never made to eat spinach. My mum gave us lots of beans on toast but never any spinach. And I still grew up big and strong.

P.S. I also know a rather good joke about the Disciples going to Mount Olive, but I think it would upset Popeye too much to repeat it here.

Remember: You score nothing for putting the goalkeeper into the back of the net.

THE PAUL GASCOIGNE STORY

PART

(**2**)

At Newcastle United Gazza soon settled into the Youth team and was made captain for the 1984-85 season, steering the side to victory in the FA Youth Cup. Newcastle beat Watford 4-1 at Vicarage Road, having been held to a goalless draw at home. Gazza was one of the scorers. At the end of that season he signed full professional forms and got his first taste of League football, coming on as a substitute at home to Queen's Park Rangers.

But it was not until the opening match of the next season, 1985-86, that he made his full debut, turning out against Southampton at the Dell. Even at this early stage – he was still only 18 – Gazza lacked nothing in confidence. 'The game went very well', he recalls. 'I got a standing ovation. I should have scored really. Peter Shilton was in goal for Southampton then. He made a great save.'

Even so, there were still moments of awe – moments that would have touched even the pawkiest teenager. 'My second game was against Liverpool, and I found myself standing right next to Kenny Dalglish and Ian Rush. I thought I must be the luckiest lad in the world.'

The Newcastle United fans, aficionados of the game, were swift to appreciate Gazza's prodigious talents and his Geordie background. He had the makings of a local hero.

Gazza's team-mates admired his skill and enjoyed his dressing-room pranks, although they were occasionally put out by the over-ambition of his play. Paul Goddard, the Newcastle centre forward, once grabbed him round the neck in exasperation when he tried one trick too many and missed a goal with only the 'keeper to beat.

Nevertheless Gazza's reputation soon reached the ears of the England management. He was picked for the national Under-21 team and in June 1987 made his debut against Morocco, scoring in the 2-0 victory.

The local hero instructs Swindon's Kieran O'Regan in Geordie country dancing.

KEEP FAT WITH GAZZA

Gazza serves up a treat
12 exciting ways to eat a Mars bar
For each serving suggestion you will need: 1 Mars bar

1   Unwrap the bar and eat it.
2   Sit down before eating the Mars bar.
3   Take the bar outside and eat it while walking down the street.
4   Eat it on the bus.
5   Put the Mars bar in the fridge for an hour before eating it.
6   Cut the Mars bar up with a knife and fork; then eat it.
7   Slice the bar thinly and put it in a sandwich.
8   Melt the Mars bar in a saucepan and then pour it over some ice cream.
9   Eat the Mars bar without unwrapping it, and then spit out the paper.
10   Eat the Mars bar with your eyes closed.
11   or standing on one leg.
12   or even with a 'novelty' baseball cap on your head.

There is, however, more to eating than Mars bars. Variety is very important in any diet.

Fruit is very good for you. I particularly like Terry's Chocolate Oranges.

Other favourite dishes include: Maltesers, Kit Kats, boiled lobster, prawn-cocktail flavoured crisps, grilled trout.

All these things should, of course, be taken in moderation.
WARNING: Think first, most footballers don't eat excessive quantities of junk food (too often).

Steve McMahon brings his faith-healing skills into play on Peter Beardsley.

THE GEORDIE-ENGLISH PHRASEBOOK

Lesson 12: At the Bar

Cud a hev us a pint o beer, please?	*Could I have a pint of beer, please?*
A sed, a'd like a pint o beer an aall.	*I said I would like a pint of beer.*
Haway man, can yuz no unnerstan English? Gissa beer!	*Can't you understand English? Give me a beer!*
Ar yuz gone in the head or summik? A wan some beer.	*Are you an idiot? I want some beer.*
Divvent you tell me t'shaddap.	*Don't you tell me to shut up.*
Ar ye startin summik, like?	*Are you looking for a punch on the nose?*
Tek that you dozy bastad!	*Take that you sleepy head!*
Hadaway an tek that tu an aall.	*It's all right, officer, I'll come quietly.*

Remember: Keep your eyes on the ball.

MANAGER SPEAK

Are parrots so very miserable? If you were 'over the moon' wouldn't you die due to lack of oxygen? Might this not be a good thing? Football managers have a language of their own, a vocabulary that is often deceptively familiar but, in fact, conceals some very different meanings. Here is an essential guide to the mysteries of Manager Speak.

'At the start of the match we'd have been happy with a draw.'
(At the start of the match no one else would have been happy with anything less than victory.)

There are no easy matches at this level.
(1-1 against a team of part-timers from Malta is not a bad result.)

It was a game of two halves.
(We may have played badly in the second half, but we played worse in the first.)

We just didn't get the breaks.
(We hit the woodwork twice.)

We made plenty of pressure.
(We had no shots at goal.)

We made a lot of chances.
(There was one shot over the bar.)

I thought we were a bit unfortunate.
(We may have lost 3-1 but we did hit the woodwork twice.)

We didn't get the run of the ball.
(We were comprehensively outplayed.)

It was just one of those games.
(*see* I thought we were a bit unfortunate.)

It was always going to be a difficult match.
(1-1 against a team of part-timers from Malta really isn't a bad result, you know.)

He's a lovely player.
(He dribbled past a defender.)

He's a great worker.
(He was fortunate not to have been sent off for a series of brutal challenges.)

He's an inspiration.
(He shouts a lot.)

He's a joy to work with.
(If he keeps playing this well I'll keep my job.)

Football is a funny old game.
(I give up.)

GAZZA'S POSTBAG

People sometimes say to me 'Gazza, do you get a lot of exciting things through the post?' And I have to tell them, yes, I do get a lot of interesting things through the post. A typical week's fan-mail might include:

- A pair of novelty boxer-shorts decorated with tiny love-hearts, from a female admirer.

- A bottle of brown ale from a considerate Geordie.

- A bill for £86 from British Telecom.

- A Mars bar (slightly squashed) from a young Spurs fan.

- A brand new Ford Fiesta (well, on closer inspection, only the chance of winning a brand new Ford Fiesta) from *Reader's Digest.*

- Another Mars bar from another young Spurs fan.

- A pair of Waterford crystal walking sticks from a very generous supporter. (These are beautiful things – and happily I don't even need walking sticks yet. I shall put them by for my retirement.)

- A free newspaper full of house adverts from the local Estate Agent. (This is an unattractive waste of paper. I shall put it by for the dustmen.)

Alan Smith, last season's top scorer, shows his skill at blow football.

Can Gazza have his cake and eat it? Paul celebrates his 21st birthday.

THE PAUL GASCOIGNE STORY

PART

It has long been one of the mysteries of the soccer world that Newcastle, a town that produces so many brilliant players and so many enthusiastic supporters, should have such an ailing football team. Gazza suggests three reasons for the club's sorry state: 'Directors, directors and directors'. Although he maintains an enormous affection for the club that gave him his first chance it was perhaps his dissatisfaction with those running the set-up that prompted him to consider a transfer at the end of the 1988 season. He had, after all, seen two of the club's other great prodigies, Peter Beardsley and Chris Waddle, move on and up.

There was much speculation about where Gazza might go. His name was linked with almost every club from Manchester United to Hamilton Academicals. But it was Tottenham Hotspur, Chris Waddle's new club, that won the race for Gascoigne's signature.

Gazza was much impressed by Terry Venables: 'He was brilliant. He seemed just like my Dad'. Unlike Paul's Dad, however, El Tel had to fork out £2 million to get Gazza. It was a transfer record and a great weight of responsibility for a 20-year-old.

Forsaking the comforts of home life in Newcastle for a hotel room in Hertfordshire was a big wrench. Chris Waddle was a great help. 'If it hadn't been for Chris,' Gazza admits, 'I might have packed it in. There were so many things I couldn't handle on my own.'

If Gazza was having a few problems so were Tottenham. The season did not start well – in fact it didn't start at all. Spurs' first game had to be cancelled at

the very last moment because construction work at White Hart Lane was incomplete. Paul's Mum and Dad had travelled south for the match.

Gazza finally made his debut for Tottenham the following weekend – back in Newcastle. The Newcastle supporters, disappointed at the defection of their hero, gave him a hard time, and pelted the pitch with Mars bars. His Mum, however, cheered him loudly. The game ended 2-2. Gazza was substituted.

Tottenham's new team and Terry Venables' new tactics were taking some time to come together. Six weeks into the League campaign Tottenham had amassed only four points; one fewer than the Star of David as some North London wags pointed out.

Gradually, however, results began to pick up (and the two penalty points deducted for the cancellation of the first fixture were restored). By the end of the season the Tottenham mean-machine was running with a semblance of smoothness, and Spurs finished fifth in the table.

Gazza's form – and his antics – swiftly endeared him to the White Hart Lane crowd. They also endeared him to Bobby Robson, the England manager. He travelled with the full England squad to Saudi Arabia – a rare chance to fly on Concorde if nothing else. He also went to Albania, but didn't play.

He did, however, make a sensational appearance when Albania visited Wembley for the return match. Coming on as a substitute for the last 22 minutes of the game, Gazza laid on one goal and scored another. His goal was a glorious solo endeavour that left the weary Albanian defence flat-footed and their 17-year-old goalkeeper helpless and prone. It was a very fine moment; the first, one hopes, of many . . .

Here's your life story. Where's my cheque?
Jack McHack

'Ee Aye Addio – we won the cutglass sherry decanter'

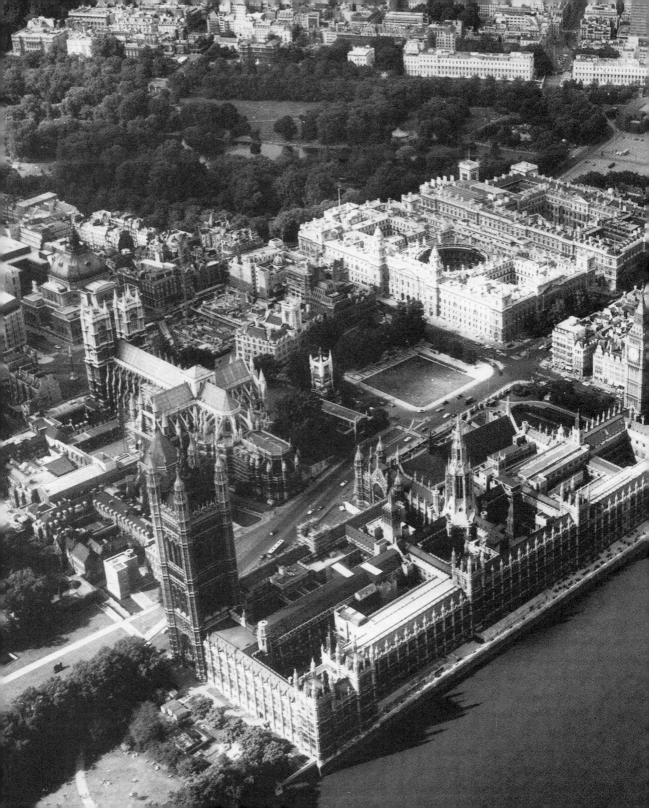

GAZZA'S GUIDE TO LONDON

I never go into town much. It's always busy whenever I go up on a shopping trip. London seems so massive. And the funny thing is that everyone seems to be competing against everyone else, whether it's walking or driving, or even going into the shops. Everyone wants to get in front of you. I'm very competitive myself, but only on the football pitch.

Remember: It is important to establish a good rapport with your team-mates.

UP FOR THE TEACUP

Gazza shows that you need more than power and pace to get round some people. Sue, the tea-lady at Tottenham's training ground, has nothing but praise for 'her lads' and for Gazza in particular.

'He's a lovely boy, a real character', she says. 'He does like his food – and anybody else's. He's particularly keen on the lasagne I make. He loves that. Recently, though, he's been on a bit of a diet. He's been very good about it. He often just has a slice of lemon in his tea now instead of milk. He's lost a lot of weight.

'But he's not always so good – he can be a terror. Once he broke one of the nice china teacups when he was larking about. I was quite cross about it. He didn't offer to replace it or anything. He just waited till I was on my own, then came in, put his head on my shoulder and said, "Am I forgiven?" The rest of the team were watching, but I couldn't go on being angry with him. I had to forgive him. He's such a charmer – he could get round anyone.

'But now he does have to drink his tea out of a plastic cup.'

THE JOKER IN THE PACK

'GAZZA IS THE LES DAWSON OF SPURS' screamed the headline. Working with me, according to Spurs' assistant manager Allan Harris, 'is like having Les Dawson at the club.'

Most people assumed that Allan was talking about my jesting ways and my stream of ad-lib gags and amusing mother-in-law jokes. But I'll let you in on a secret. I don't have a mother-in-law. I'm not even married.

It seems that Allan Harris's comments – made in the *Sun* 'newspaper' at the end of last year – were in fact a reference to Les Dawson's little-known skill as a football player.

Big Les, famous for his appearances on TV's *Blankety Blank* 'show', could have been a top-class international footballer, a player in the Gazza mould.

'Mind you,' says a respected sport and fitness expert, 'to make the grade in today's competitive soccer world he would have to lose a bit of weight and work hard to improve his close ball control. His running off the ball is always intelligent, but he must look to get into
the box more often.'

Les Dawson displays his uncanny sense of balance.

At the moment the man they sometimes call the 'fat white Pele' is content with his television work and club appearances. According to his agent he has no plans to return to the football field.

Paul Gascoigne, however, is considering a tour of working men's clubs in the North of England.

Football may well be 'a funny old game', but just *how* funny and *how* old is it? The chance discovery of the Comedy XI team-card (printed below) suggests that it is very old, if nothing else.

THE COMEDY XI

Les Dawson,
Laurel, Hardy,
Sgt Bilko, Gazza,
Billy Connolly, Abbott,
Jerry Lewis, Greavsie,
Charlie Chaplin, Costello

The Manageress:
Dame Edna Everage

'Stan' Waddle and 'Ollie' Gascoigne discuss the serious business of football.

SUPERSTITIONS

I'm not at all superstitious. Well, not very superstitious. But I don't like going out on to the pitch last at the start of a match. Gary Lineker doesn't mind being last out – in fact I think he likes it. It's another good thing about having him on the team.

But apart from not being last out of the tunnel I don't have any superstitions. Some players always put their kit on in the same order – socks, shorts and then their shirt. But I can't be bothered with all that; I'd never remember it.

Of course, I don't walk under ladders. And I don't like seeing black cats or pennies.

So, apart from not coming out on to the pitch last, walking under ladders, meeting black cats and seeing pennies, I really don't have any superstitions at all. I'm lucky like that.

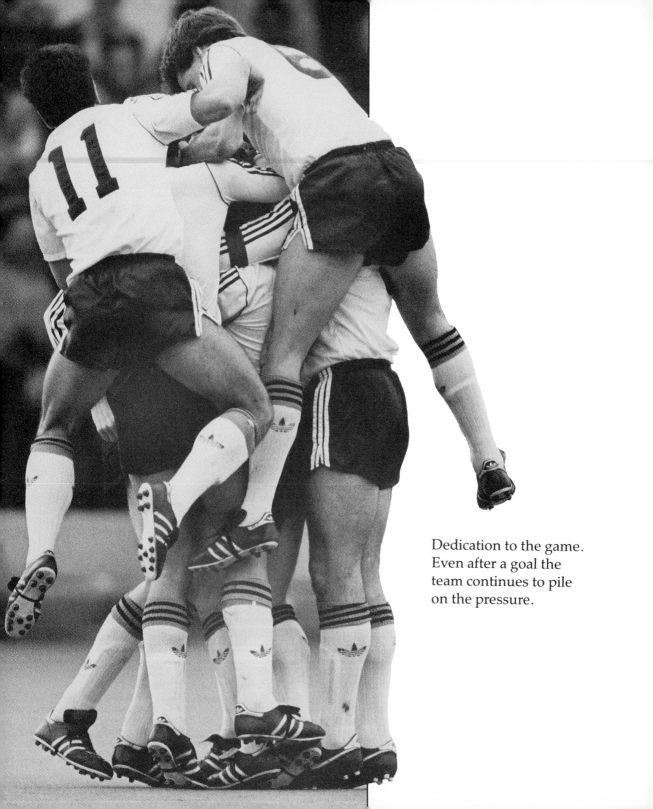

Dedication to the game.
Even after a goal the
team continues to pile
on the pressure.

TOP TEAMS 1

ARSENAL

Tottenham haven't won a North London derby for a few years, so we will be looking to do well against the old enemy this time around. Last season we played a thriller at White Hart Lane. I scored a goal, but lost my boot. And although Chris Waddle scored another goal we lost the match 2-3. I missed the return game at Highbury.

This season it will be even harder. Arsenal are a skilful team, especially in midfield, and they always work very hard. To add to that they'll be on a real high after winning the Championship in such dramatic style at the end of the 1988-89 season.

Putting the sock back into soccer: Gazza scores against Arsenal.

Remember: Don't
make a daft pop
record (well, not
too often).

STARS OF THE FUTURE 1

When I go back home to Newcastle I sometimes help coach the youngsters there. There are some great new players coming through.

LEE CLARKE is a teenager in the Reserves at Newcastle United. He may even have had an outing with the first team by now. He is a great talent with neat ball control.

TOMMY HERRING is another 16-year-old breaking into the Newcastle United side. He has a lot of skill and is definitely worth watching out for.

My other favourite young player is **PAUL WHARTON**, the son of United's Kenny Wharton. Paul is only 11 but he's absolutely brilliant – nippy, skilful and very competitive. He's coached by Stan Nixon at the Newcastle United School of Excellence and he certainly should achieve excellence, too.

THE WISDOM OF THE TERRACES

There's only one
Gary Mabbutt

Tottenham supporters[1]

Oh Mirandinha
He's not from Argentina
He's from Brazil
He's xxxxing brill

*Newcastle United
supporters*

---

[1] There are, in fact, at least four people of that name living in the London area alone.

[2] A famous old chant, so it must be true. I'm sure everyone has already forgotten Arsenal's 'boring' last-minute winner in last season's championship decider. Yawn.

[3] This is sung to the tune of Rod Stewart's 'Sailing' which makes it even more depressing.

GAZZA'S FASHION TIPS

It's got to be white. White, with maybe just a hint of blue, is definitely the 'look' for this season. It's a colour that suits the fuller figure, and it always stands out in the crowd.

Stripes, I am afraid, are rather *passé*.

Top model Gary Lineker shows off the new 'modo bianco'.

GAZZA'S GUIDE
TO THE NIGHT-SPOTS
OF ALBANIA

ARE YOU ONE OF SOCCER'S HARD MEN?

Are you as tough as you pretend to be? Do you eat creative midfield players for breakfast or do you prefer cornflakes? The following quiz will sort out the Whitesides from the Yellow Bellies.

1 When you go to the hairdresser's do you ask for:
a) A number one?
b) A perm?
c) A lobotomy?

2 An early bath is:
a) A morning ablution
b) A Roman spa
c) A satisfactory end to a football match

3 As a child did you admire:
a) 'Bomber' Harris?
b) 'Chopper' Harris?
c) Rolf Harris?

4 John Barnes is threatening to take the ball past you on the left wing. Do you:
a) Rob the ball from his very feet and play a thoughtful through pass to one of your own forwards
b) Hoof the ball into the stands
c) Hoof John Barnes into the stands

5 A stud is:
a) A breeding stable for racehorses
b) A bloke with a hairy chest
c) Something you rake down an opponent's back

6 When relaxing at home do you:
a) Listen to Dire Straits?
b) Read *Shoot* magazine?
c) Pull the legs off insects?

7 At a corner kick you use your head for:
a) Thinking
b) Flicking the ball on at the near post
c) Butting the goalkeeper

8 When going in for a challenge do you keep:
a) Your eye on the ball?
b) Your eye on the opponent?
c) Your hand on the opponent's balls?

9 Norman Whiteside is:
a) A fine and competitive midfield player
b) A breed of cow from northern France
c) Too rough by half

10 After 12 pints of lager you feel like:
a) Being sick
b) Going for a piss
c) Having another lager

Your score: **1**a – 2, b – 0, c – 5; **2**a – 0, b – 0, c – 3; **3**a – 0, b – 4, c – –2; **4**a – 0, b – 1, c – 3; **5**a – 0, b – 1, c – 3; **6**a – –8, b – –2, c – 4; **7**a – –2, b – 0, c – 4; **8**a – 0, b – 0, c – 3; **9**a – 1, b – 0, c – 0; **10**a – –2, b – 0, c – 3.

IF YOU SCORED LESS THAN 5: Nancy! You have less bottle than a Muslim minibar. What are you doing playing football at all? Remember, it is a man's game played by real men; skill and thought have nothing to do with it. So push off back to France Mr 'so called' Glenn Hoddle.

IF YOU SCORED MORE THAN 5: You have the makings of a professional footballer. You should do well in the English League.

IF YOU CAN'T READ THE QUESTIONNAIRE: Well, there's not much point in writing any of this for you, is there? But have you considered signing for Wimbledon? I hear they are looking to 'strengthen' their midfield.

GAZZA'S GALLERY OF GRIZZLIES

REMI MOSES, who used to play for Manchester United, was everywhere. He was a very tough player.

VINNY JONES nearly got my family allowance. He may be hard, but that's just the way he plays. He once said in the papers that he wants to be the next Trevor Brooking – the grannies' favourite!

PAUL McGRATH is a real terrier. He's very difficult to get past.

Handball. Vinny Jones takes close marking to extremes in a gripping encounter at Plough Lane.

Remember: Always keep the ball(s) covered.

IS ELVIS PRESLEY ALIVE AND WELL AND PLAYING FOR TOTTENHAM HOTSPUR?

Since Elvis's 'death' in 1977 many of his fans have become convinced that the 'King' of Rock 'n' Roll did not in fact die and that he is still alive, living a new life as someone else. It has been suggested that Elvis, unable to face the enormous pressures of his musical fame, staged his own 'funeral' and then adopted a new identity.

But what new identity did he choose? Some think he became a petrol pump attendant in Tulsa, others claim to have discovered him working as the manager of a trailer park on the outskirts of Cleethorpes (Arizona).

Now, however, it seems that Elvis may be living in Britain, playing football for a famous First Division club under the pseudonym 'Paul Gascoigne'.

The claim seems incredible but the evidence is almost impossible to deny. Fact: 'Paul' admits that he likes 'singing'. Fact: he has a very expensive Japanese karaoke machine in his house and often sings along to Elvis's 'hits'. I love "Jailhouse Rock" ', he says, 'and all Elvis's faster songs; they really get me motivated.'

And if this 'coincidence' isn't strange enough, there is the uncanny fact that 'Paul Gascoigne' was almost unknown before 1977, the year of Elvis's death.

Add to this the striking physical resemblance between the two heart-throbs and we must be left wondering whether they might not be one and the same person. The truth, after all, is often stranger than fiction.

Elvis as he was in the 1970s . . .

. . . 'Gazza' as he appears today. Why do they both have their mouths open?

MY HEROES

Here I pick my favourite players and, by one of those strange coincidences that often happen in books, they all come from Newcastle, or from just down the road. Maybe they put something in the water up there . . .

CHRIS WADDLE is my favourite at the moment. He has been great, especially this last year, when things have been quite tough. I don't think you really appreciate anyone properly until you've actually been there playing in the same side with them. Chris is fantastic; very skilful. Also he's got a great haircut. I'm thinking of having my hair shaved at the sides, cut very short on top and left long at the back. I think the 'Chris Waddle look' is very stylish . . .

PETER BEARDSLEY is another outstanding player. I played with Peter for a season and a half at Newcastle and it was a great education. I was disappointed to see him leave, but that's life, you know. And anyway it's good to see Geordie lads doing well.

BRYAN ROBSON is another Geordie. He's from Chester-le-Street. He is the most difficult person there is to play against in midfield. I really like Bryan Robson. Sometimes I think perhaps I give him too much respect, but the next time I play against him I won't. He's a very good footballer. I would like to play against Bryan every week because he's a top-class player – well, he's fantastic isn't he? – and playing against him makes my game better.

You've got to hand it to Peter – he's brilliant.

THE MEN IN BLACK

Referees often come in for a lot of stick. But I think most of them do a difficult job very well. I get on well with nearly all of them. They don't mind me larking about – some of them even say they like it.

Obviously, I do sometimes get into trouble. I have a very quick temper. But I think as I grow older I'll wear it down. I'm certainly working at it.

And refs nowadays are much more cautious than they used to be. If there is an incident they tend to step back and think about it before getting the book out.

So let's hear it for the smallest team on the field. 'COME ON YOU BLACKS!'

Why didn't you go at half-time like everybody else?

Remember: Don't get up the referee's nose.

WHAT'S IN A NAME 2

Playing football you get used to being called by a nickname. I've been known as Gazza since I was a bairn (see page 12). It's not a bad name.

Paul Walsh gets called Janice because of his long hair. And Paul Allen is sometimes called Ollie, though I'm not sure quite why.

Steve Sedgley is known as E.T. And it's not because he can play 'out of this world', it's because his neck is so long he looks just like the Extra Terrestrial. Ho ho.

Steve Sedgley — 'phone home.

Gazza takes a shot from the edge of the area.

TOP TEAMS 2

LIVERPOOL

Ever since I've been playing football Liverpool have been at the top. No matter who wins the Championship (and it is usually Liverpool), Liverpool are always the team to beat; the team to measure yourself against. Their consistency is incredible.

The fixtures against Liverpool are always exhausting. They pass and move the whole time; they make it very hard for you. They get rid of the ball so quickly you have no chance to make a tackle. Once you have lost the ball against Liverpool it is very difficult to get it back.

They may have some star players, like Peter Beardsley and John Barnes, but the whole team fits together so well. It's awesome.

Steve McMahon and colleagues prove that they'll never walk alone.

Remember: Try to confuse the opposition.

IMPROVE YOUR INTERVIEW TECHNIQUE

Playing football may be pretty tiring but dealing with the press is a really exhausting sport.

THE POST-MATCH INTERVIEW

You have just struggled off the pitch after a punishing 90 minutes of fiercely competitive football when you are approached by a man in a sheepskin coat. He is brandishing a microphone.

What the interviewer says:
What was it like out there? It looked like a hard match.

What you want to say:
Aye, a've been kickt black an' blu by them bastards. But a did manage to get in a bit o' reetaliation, an' aal.

What you do say:
Yes, Brian, it was tough out there; very competitive.

You scored a goal

What the interviewer says:
Gazza, tell us a bit about that second goal.

What you want to say:
Aw man, gee'z a break. A'm knackered oot, a'm cold and a'm covered i' mud. A jus wanna go an' hev me bath, like.

What you do say:
Well, Chris put in a great ball from the left. I just put my foot out and there it was, in the back of the net.

Your team have just won an important cup match; you played a blinder and scored the winning goal

What the interviewer says:
That was a great performance, Paul. Are you pleased with the way it went?

What you want to say:
Pleased!?! Yu's gotta be jokin'. O' course a'm pleased! We won the game an' aal. It wuz greet, man.

What you do say:
Aye, Martin, I'm well pleased.

LEFT Jim Rosenthal, television's 'Mr Cool', takes the temperature at Wembley as Cup final fever grips the stadium.

RIGHT Brian Moore demonstrates the new Remington razor: a smart appearance is vital for television work.

THE DAWN RAID

You are coming out of a nightclub in the early hours of Sunday morning, you have a girl on your arm. Suddenly a reporter from the tabloid press springs out of the shadows.

What the interviewer says:
Oi Gazza, what are you up to then? Who's the girl?

What you want to say:
Gan eesy will yer, man. A've jus been fer a neet oot with me gal. There's nowt wrong wi' that is there, yer daft tike?

What you do say:
No comment.

THE SILLY QUESTION

You are being interviewed for a club fanzine and are talking about your Japanese 'singing machine'.

What the interviewer says:
So, what do you do with your 'singing machine'?

What you want to say:
Play golf.

What you do say:
Play golf.

THE TWO-BALL GAME

Bobby Robson is often unfairly criticised for neglecting tactical innovations. But he has now made a significant contribution of his own to the playing of Association Football. After England's game against Albania at Wembley he suggested that henceforth England should play with two footballs, one for me and another for the rest of the team. FIFA are still considering the proposal.

Spurs' Philip Gray and Alvin Martin of West Ham struggle with the concept of the two-ball game.

ADVICE TO THE YOUNG

I'm sometimes asked for advice on how to become a successful footballer. As if I would know the answer! But if you do want to succeed there is no alternative but to listen and learn, and to work very hard.

You should listen to those who know about the game, and learn from them. You can also learn a great deal by playing against good players. Pit yourself against the best. When you are on the pitch always want to have the ball. And when you're not playing a match, keep practising.

When I was a kid I was always with a ball – a football, a tennis ball, anything – kicking it about, learning to control it, trying to juggle it. There is no substitute for practice.

You do, however, also need a bit of luck. So it is advisable not to wander under ladders or let black cats cross your path (see page 54).

Remember: Most footballers don't smoke.

TOP TEAMS 3

MANCHESTER UNITED

Although they have had some disappointing seasons of late, Manchester United are still one of the biggest clubs in football.

A match against United is always a big occasion, and always a taxing one. Any team with Bryan Robson in it is going to be difficult to do well against. And now United have strengthened their midfield still further by buying Neil Webb, Mike Phelan and Paul Ince. That must give them one of the strongest midfields in the League.

On top of that the new chairman, Michael Knighton, seems to have created a fresh wave of expectation and enthusiasm. They will be looking to do well in 1989-90.

Chairman Michael Knighton reaches for the skies.

THE PERILS OF BEING A FOOTBALLER 2

MAGICIANS

I once went with the Tottenham team to a charity event which boasted a magician as part of the entertainment. Early on in his act he invited me up on the stage and asked me to give him my watch – a brand new gold Rolex.

I was a bit reluctant but I handed it over. He took it in his hand, wrapped it up in a silk handkerchief, and then proceeded to smash it to pieces with a large hammer. I was stunned. But he didn't offer any explanation, he just put the little bundle to one side and told me to go back to my seat. Everyone laughed. Bastards.

Throughout the rest of the show I sat there waiting for him to come back to me with my watch. But he seemed to be ignoring me. Card tricks, disappearing rabbits, re-appearing bottles; the show went on for over an hour. (Not of course that I had a watch to time it with.)

I was getting really anxious when the conjurer finally said, 'Oh, I almost forgot; can the gentleman whose watch I borrowed please come back up on to the stage'. I ran straight up. He took hold of the bundled handkerchief, waved his wand over it and then opened it up. There was a cheap-looking watch inside. 'Is that your watch, sir?' he asked.

'No it isn't,' I told him. 'Mine is a Rolex.'

'Ah ha,' said the magician. Then from his table he picked up a large fruit cake and a knife. 'Perhaps you would be so kind, then, as to slice this fruit cake in half?' I took the knife and cut right through the cake. It fell into two halves. And what do you think I saw inside the cake?

(Continued overleaf)

Nuts and raisins.

Remember: Don't let
success go to your
head.

THE LURE OF THE CONTINENT

We were all very sad to see Chris Waddle go off to Marseilles. He loved Tottenham and wanted to play for them. That's why he had recently signed a long contract. But when such a big offer was made for him then obviously both he and the club had to reconsider.

Although he is missed by the Tottenham players just as much as he is by the Tottenham fans, we will, I'm sure, manage without him. And, of course, we all wish him the best of luck in France.

I've never really thought about playing in Europe myself. I'm very happy at Tottenham and although I do love pasta, Sue, the tea-lady here, makes such a good lasagne that there's no need to go all the way to Europe.

Remember: Stick close to your man.

MYSTERIES OF THE GAME No 5

WHY ARE SO MANY OF THE TOTTENHAM TEAM CALLED PAUL?

Paul Stewart	Pope John Paul II
Paul Gascoigne	Paul Moran
Paul Walsh	Paul Mabbutt
Paul Allen	Paul Lineker

Is it the result of an international conspiracy by people with the Christian name Paul?

Is it due to the manager, Paul Venables', personal whim?

Is it part of a fiendishly clever attempt to confuse other teams?

Is it just a coincidence?

Paul Moran

New signing Paul Lineker is shown off by 'El Paul' Venables.

STARS OF THE FUTURE 2

Tottenham has a very good youth policy and there are some exciting young home-grown players rising through the ranks.

Big **GUY BUTTERS** is going to be a very accomplished central defender. He was thrown in at the deep end last season and has coped brilliantly. He reads the game well and stays cool under pressure.

VINNY SAMWAYS should become a star. He is still establishing himself in the first team, but at Tottenham they have always loved skilful midfield players and Vinny is just that.

IAN HENDON, a young centre-half in the Reserves, is also very impressive. We will all be hearing a lot more about him, I'm sure.

Guy Butters.

Remember: Always look
on the bright side.